I0569266

# HEALING (of) HEARTS

BY AXEL JORDAN

VOL. 1

to the seekers, the dreamers, and the healers—
this book is for you.

for those navigating the quiet storms within,
for those rising again after the fall,
and for those learning to love themselves a little more each day—
may these words bring you comfort, hope, and the reminder
that healing begins in the heart.

with gratitude for your courage and light,
this is dedicated to your journey.

contents

# INTRODUCTION

Within these pages lies a heartfelt companion for anyone seeking solace, growth, and inner peace. Filled with inspiring short stories, gentle poems, and letters of encouragement, this book invites you to explore themes of resilience, self-love, growth, forgiveness, hope, and acceptance. Each chapter guides you through powerful reflections and prompts that nurture self-discovery and help you embrace life's challenges with grace and courage.

This book is more than a collection; it's a reminder that you are never alone on your journey. Whether you're looking to heal old wounds or simply find comfort in the everyday moments, HEALING (of) HEARTS offers a beacon of hope and gentle guidance for each step forward.

Each chapter aims to lead you toward a deeper understanding of yourself, to inspire personal growth, and to empower you to continue forward with resilience, self-love, growth, forgiveness, hope, and acceptance. Through each step, you'll be equipped with tools to embrace life's journey with openness and courage, ready to face whatever lies ahead.

Allow yourself to be uplifted, inspired, and transformed. Embrace who you are and all that you are becoming.

# RESILIENCE

*HEALING (of) HEARTS*

Resilience is the ability to rise after each fall, to find strength within, even when life's challenges feel insurmountable. This chapter provides an encouraging foundation, sharing stories and reflections on facing hardship with courage and determination. Through the guidance offered here, you'll discover that resilience is not about never falling, but about the will to stand back up each time. By the chapter's end, you'll feel empowered to embrace life's difficulties with newfound strength, knowing you have the ability to navigate whatever comes your way.

In the quiet strength that
rises after every fall,
we learn the depth
of our courage and the
power of our spirit.

"The Climb Back"

Elena sat on the edge of her bed, staring at the rejection letter in her hands. It was the third time this month. After years of putting her heart into her career and reaching for her dreams, things had fallen apart. Her company downsized, her savings dwindled, and the endless job applications had worn her spirit thin.

But today, as she looked at the letter, something shifted. She remembered her grandmother's words: "When life throws you down, don't stand back up the same. Stand back up stronger." Elena took a deep breath, wiping away her tears. She decided to take a different approach—she'd use this time to sharpen her skills, reach out to old mentors, and focus on projects she'd always wanted to pursue but never had time for.

Months later, a job offer arrived, but by then, she was no longer the same person who had felt defeated. She was resilient, with a renewed sense of purpose. Elena realized that life's setbacks had taught her to stand up stronger, transforming each fall into a new opportunity.

Even in your weakest moments,
you hold the power to rise.
Trust in your strength;
it's always there, even when hidden.

"Unbreakable"

Beneath the weight of crashing waves,
I am rooted, unafraid.
Though storms may rage, I stand, I stay,
With every blow, I find my way.
The world may shake, the skies may roar,
Yet in my core, I am much more.
Unbreakable, fierce, and strong,
I rise again, where I belong.

dearest beauty,

i know the weight of hard times and the way they can make you feel as if you've lost your footing. Life's challenges sometimes feel like they're too much to bear. But here's the truth: you're stronger than you know.

resilience doesn't mean life gets easier or that setbacks won't happen. It means you have the power to face each moment with courage, no matter how many times you fall. You get to stand back up, each time with more strength, wisdom, and grace.

in those moments of hardship, remember to be kind to yourself. Embrace your journey and know that every experience, no matter how painful, is shaping you into someone extraordinary. Trust in your resilience, and know that every step forward—no matter how small—is proof of your strength.

with courage,

the you thats past this

Take a moment to think about a time in your life when you faced a difficult situation and came out stronger.
What inner strengths or resources did you discover?
How did this experience shape you?

_____

_____

_____

As you move on your journey, remember that resilience is a lifelong companion. It's the quiet but unwavering presence within you, guiding you through both the calm and the storm. Moving forward isn't about having all the answers or a perfectly paved path. It's about trusting yourself enough to face each step with courage, even when the way is uncertain.

As you grow, you may face new obstacles but each will reveal another layer of strength within you. Embrace these moments with an open heart, and remember that you have everything you need to keep going, to keep rising, and to continue building a life of purpose and meaning.

Hold close the power of resilience, and know that whatever comes, you will face it—and you will rise.

Write down a personal mantra or affirmation that speaks to your strength and resilience. Use this mantra as a reminder whenever you face challenges.

Try repeating it to yourself daily for the next week to see how it affects your mindset.

_____

_____

_____

True resilience is not in never falling
but in always choosing to rise.

"The Rising Tide"

Sam had always been drawn to the ocean, but on this particular day, he felt as though he was drowning in life's storms. His business was struggling, and he was unsure if he could keep it afloat. As he sat on the beach, watching the waves crash and recede, he noticed a piece of driftwood that remained on the shore no matter how many times the waves pulled it back.

Inspired, Sam thought of all the times he'd felt defeated but had continued forward anyway. That piece of driftwood became a symbol of his own strength —the power to remain standing, even when the tide seemed too strong. The challenges didn't stop, but Sam learned to adapt, to float when he couldn't swim, and to embrace the storms with the same resilience as the driftwood on the shore. He knew that, just like the ocean, his spirit was unbreakable.

Resilience isn't about never falling.
It's about having the courage to stand
back up each time, a little wiser
and a little stronger.

you,

life can sometimes feel like an unending series of waves, each one pulling you down. In these moments, resilience may feel distant. But know this: you hold within you an extraordinary ability to rise, to stand back up each time, no matter the depth of the struggle.

resilience is not about perfection or having all the answers. It's about the simple choice to keep going, to adapt, and to find your footing again, even if it feels shaky. Remember, every time you rise, you grow stronger, wiser, and more capable.

take heart in the strength you've shown in the past, and let it remind you that you can face whatever comes. You are a force of resilience, a testament to the power of the human spirit.

with faith in you,

me

"Rise Again"

With every fall, I rise once more,
My heart a wave upon the shore.
In tides that pull, in storms that wane,
I find the strength to rise again.

I am the wind, the sea, the stone,
I stand, resilient and not alone.
Through every trial, fierce and strong,
I am the storm, where I belong.

Think about a challenging time in your life that helped shape who you are today. How did you grow from that experience, and what strengths did you discover within yourself?

_____

_____

_____

Create a small ritual to honor your resilience. This could be lighting a candle, repeating an empowering mantra, or writing a list of strengths that help you face difficult times.

What is that ritual?

_____

_____

_____

Return to this ritual whenever you need a reminder of your inner strength.

Resilience is a journey, a steady pulse that moves you forward through both the calm and the storms. Moving forward, remember that resilience doesn't erase hardship; it transforms it. It's a powerful guide that helps you face life's waves with a heart that is open, strong, and unwavering.

As you embrace each new step, know that resilience will be your companion, whispering encouragement when the way feels unclear. Trust in your capacity to rise and face each moment with strength, knowing you are more capable than you once believed.

Let resilience be the foundation upon which you build a life filled with courage, meaning, and purpose. Step forward with a quiet confidence, knowing you are both the wave and the shore, ready to face whatever comes.

"The Phoenix Within"

After a sudden layoff, Leo found himself struggling to make ends meet. Job rejections piled up, and with each one, his self-worth took a hit. He felt as though he'd lost everything, and his sense of identity wavered. One evening, as he scrolled through old photos, he stumbled upon a picture of a small clay phoenix he'd made as a child—a symbol of rebirth from the ashes.

Inspired, Leo decided to take a new approach. Instead of seeing himself as defeated, he chose to view this moment as a chance to rise anew. He started a small freelance project, rediscovered his creative side, and built himself back up, one small victory at a time. Leo realized that resilience was not just about enduring; it was about embracing the opportunity to recreate himself. Like the phoenix, he found strength in rising from his own ashes, stronger than before.

Resilience is not just strength;
it is the grace to adapt
and the courage to keep
moving forward.

"Strength to Bend"

In winds that test, I bend, not break,
With roots that hold, though branches shake.
I find my way, despite the storm,
Resilience keeps my spirit warm.

Though battered leaves may fall away,
My core remains, through night and day.
For in my soul, there's strength to mend,
In every storm, I learn to bend.

Think about a person or experience that helped shape your resilience. What did this experience teach you, and how has it contributed to the person you are today?

_____

_____

_____

you,

resilience is not just the ability to withstand hardship; it's the quiet decision to keep going, to trust that you can handle whatever life brings. In every challenge, there is an opportunity to learn more about yourself, to discover inner strengths you never knew you had.

remember, resilience is also about kindness—kindness to yourself as you navigate tough times. It's okay to rest, to stumble, and to feel uncertain. Each time you choose to rise, you build a deeper foundation of courage and wisdom.

trust in your journey, knowing that you have the resilience to not only survive but to thrive. You are growing, even when it feels like you're standing still. Keep going with faith and patience, and know that your strength is a light guiding you forward.

with unwavering support,

your best friend

Each day for a week, write down one small victory, no matter how minor it may seem. Let this daily practice remind you of your resilience and show you that progress is being made, even in small steps.

Day 1: _____

Day 2: _____

Day 3: _____

Day 4: _____

Day 5: _____

Day 6: _____

Day 7: _____

Resilience is the grace to endure and adapt, the inner strength to rise again and again. Moving forward, let resilience be your steady anchor, helping you to navigate life's uncertainties with courage and patience. Know that resilience is a skill, one that grows with each experience, and that each step strengthens the foundation beneath you.

As you continue on this path, allow resilience to be a quiet source of strength, reminding you of the power within. You are capable of weathering any storm, finding new beginnings in each challenge. Move forward with confidence, trusting in your resilience and the journey that lies ahead.

# SELF-LOVE

*HEALING (of) HEARTS*

Self-love is the core of all healing and growth, yet it's often the most difficult to cultivate. This chapter invites you to explore the beauty and importance of accepting yourself fully, flaws and all. Through heartfelt letters, affirmations, and reflective prompts, you'll be encouraged to shift your perspective and see yourself with kindness. The goal is to leave this chapter with a stronger, more compassionate relationship with yourself, understanding that you are worthy of love simply for being who you are.

To honor yourself is
not an act of vanity;
it is an act of courage.

Self-love is the foundation
of all growth.

"The Mirror's Reflection"

Amara spent years avoiding mirrors. Every time she caught her reflection, a cascade of criticism followed. She scrutinized every flaw, every imperfection. It was as if she couldn't see beyond the surface to the person she truly was.

One day, at a friend's encouragement, Amara stood in front of the mirror and decided to find one thing she liked about herself. Her eyes landed on her hands, hands that had painted, written, and comforted. She whispered, "These hands have created beauty and held loved ones."

Slowly, Amara began to see herself through a different lens. Every morning, she'd stand before the mirror and say something kind—sometimes it was her compassion, other times her strength. Over time, the criticism softened, replaced by appreciation and love. She realized she was enough, just as she was, imperfections and all.

"Whole"

I am not pieces scattered and small,
I am whole, complete, and tall.
With every scar, every line,
I am perfectly, imperfectly mine.
No need to hide, no need to prove,
For I am worthy, I am true.
I hold myself, my heart, my soul,
For in my being, I am whole.

dear lil me,

there is something incredibly powerful about loving yourself exactly as you are. It's an act of bravery, a quiet but bold declaration that you are worthy of your own love. Self-love is a journey, not a destination—it takes time, patience, and a gentle heart.

when you look at yourself, remember that you are not just the sum of your flaws. You are your dreams, your kindness, your resilience, and so much more. Take moments to honor the incredible person you are becoming. Stand up for yourself, prioritize your needs, and let go of the urge to be perfect.

loving yourself doesn't mean you're done growing; it means you embrace each step with compassion. Know that you are enough, and that you deserve the same love and respect that you so freely give to others.

with love,

big me

You are deserving of
your own kindness.

Speak to yourself as
you would to someone
you love deeply.

Think about an aspect of yourself that you tend to criticize.

Consider how you would speak to a friend who expressed the same thoughts. Can you extend that same kindness and understanding to yourself?

Each morning for the next week, look in the mirror and say one kind thing to yourself.
It could be something physical, emotional, or even a strength you admire.
Notice how this small ritual begins to shift your perspective.

Day 1: _____

Day 2: _____

Day 3: _____

Day 4: _____

Day 5: _____

Day 6: _____

Day 7: _____

Walking the Path of Self-Love

Self-love is a commitment to honoring yourself through life's journey. It's not about reaching a place of perfection; it's about appreciating yourself as you are while embracing the potential for growth. Moving forward, remember to be gentle with yourself, to offer patience in moments of doubt, and to hold yourself with the same compassion you would offer someone you deeply love.

Self-love builds the foundation for every other relationship, including the one with yourself. As you walk this path, know that it's okay to falter, to question, and to rise again with greater compassion. Trust in your worth and remember that your journey is uniquely yours, valuable and meaningful.

Embrace the beauty of who you are, and continue to walk forward with love—for yourself and for all that you are becoming.

To truly love oneself is to honor every part,
even the pieces we keep hidden.

"A Journey Within"

Lena spent years seeking validation from others, always trying to be what she thought people wanted her to be. She found herself exhausted and unfulfilled, as every attempt to please others left her feeling more distant from herself. One day, a friend gifted her a journal, encouraging her to write just for herself. At first, she hesitated, fearing what she might find.

But as she began to write, something remarkable happened. Lena uncovered parts of herself she hadn't allowed herself to see—dreams she had buried, strengths she had dismissed, and moments of joy she'd forgotten. She realized that self-love wasn't about becoming something new; it was about uncovering the beauty that was already there. Lena's journey within taught her that true fulfillment comes from embracing her authentic self, without judgment or comparison.

There's something profoundly beautiful about loving yourself exactly as you are. It means accepting not only the parts of you that shine but also those that feel less certain. Self-love is not an endpoint but a journey, a commitment to holding yourself with compassion through every season.

Remember that you are worthy of your own love, not for what you do or achieve, but simply for who you are. Embrace yourself with the same kindness you'd show a dear friend. Take time to nurture your spirit, to celebrate your strengths, and to forgive your flaws.

You are a unique and irreplaceable part of this world, and no one else can bring what you do. Love yourself fully, knowing that this love will open doors to endless possibilities.

"In My Own Hands"

I hold myself with gentle care,
In my own hands, my heart laid bare.
No need for masks, no need to hide,
For I am whole, deep and wide.

Each flaw, each scar, a story told,
In every part, I find my gold.
With love I stand, a friend to me,
For in my heart, I am free.

Celebrate the small victories -
the moments of self-care and compassion.
Self-love is a journey, and each step matters.

Consider an aspect of yourself that you've struggled to embrace. Reflect on how this part of you adds to your uniqueness.

How might accepting it bring you closer to a place of inner peace?

_____

_____

_____

Walking the Path of Self-Love

Self-love is a quiet but powerful force, one that fuels every other part of your life. As you continue forward, remember that loving yourself is not about perfection; it's about seeing yourself with compassion and celebrating the unique person you are.

Moving forward, embrace self-love as a lifelong journey, a choice you make each day. Let it remind you of your inherent worth and the value you bring to the world simply by being you. The more you love yourself, the more you'll open your heart to life, relationships, and growth.

Step forward with confidence, knowing that self-love will carry you through all that lies ahead. Embrace your journey, and remember that you are already enough, just as you are.

Every day for the next week, write down one thing you appreciate about yourself.

Whether it's a quality, a small achievement, or a positive thought, let this practice help you cultivate a deeper connection to self-love.

Day 1: _____

Day 2: _____

Day 3: _____

Day 4: _____

Day 5: _____

Day 6: _____

Day 7: _____

Self-love is the gentle act of giving
yourself the kindness you
freely offer to others.

"Learning to Be Enough"

Allison had always been her own toughest critic. No matter what she achieved, she'd quickly brush it aside, setting her sights on the next goal. One day, after a particularly exhausting week, she found herself sitting in a small cafe, watching people around her laughing and relaxing. She wondered how they seemed so at ease, so content with just being.

That day, she made a promise to herself: she would practice being enough, just as she was. Allison started by writing herself small notes, simple reminders that she was worthy of rest, of praise, of kindness. With each note, she felt a little more whole. Over time, she discovered that self-love wasn't a grand declaration but a daily commitment to honoring herself. She learned to let go of perfection, embracing herself as beautifully, imperfectly enough.

"Heart Full of Grace"

I meet myself with gentle eyes,
With grace that softens self-made lies.

No more to prove, no need to change,
In every flaw, my heart remains.

I am my friend, my truest guide,
Through love I walk, my arms open wide.

For I am whole, just as I stand,
A heart full of grace, held in my hand.

Self-love is one of the greatest gifts you can give yourself, a foundation for all growth and healing. It's not about pride or vanity; it's about honoring who you are, right here and now. Self-love means offering yourself the patience, understanding, and forgiveness that you so readily give to others.

Remember, you are worthy of your own kindness, not because of what you achieve or how you look, but simply because you are. Take time to embrace yourself fully, to see yourself with the compassion you deserve. Self-love is a journey, a gentle practice that brings you closer to your true self each day.

Allow yourself to rest in the knowledge that you are enough. You are deserving of love, especially your own.

Think of a recent moment when you were hard on yourself.

What would it look like to approach yourself with kindness
instead?
How might this shift your perspective?

_____

_____

_____

This week, spend a few moments each morning looking in the mirror and saying one kind thing about yourself. It could be about a personal quality, a strength, or simply a word of encouragement. Write each down and stick to your mirror. The words to yourself are important so choose them kindly.

Every day for the next week, see how your kind words to yourself grows.

Allow this moment to deepen your connection to self-love.

Embracing Self-Love Daily

Self-love is not a destination but a journey, one that deepens as you continue to show up for yourself each day. Moving forward, let self-love be your steady companion, reminding you of your worth and the importance of honoring who you are. Let go of the need to be perfect, and embrace each part of yourself with compassion.

As you walk this path, trust that self-love is a guiding light, bringing clarity, strength, and peace. Embrace each step, knowing that you are enough, just as you are. Allow self-love to open your heart to the beauty of your own journey, and let it lead you toward a life filled with acceptance and joy.

>>>

# HEALING (of) HEARTS

# GROWTH

# HEALING (of) HEARTS

Growth is an ongoing journey, a process of continuous becoming. In this chapter, you'll find stories that illustrate the power of stepping outside your comfort zone, embracing change, and expanding your potential. Through these insights, you'll learn to view growth as an evolving journey rather than a destination, filled with valuable lessons along the way. By the end, you'll be inspired to welcome growth with curiosity and courage, ready to continue building a life aligned with your true self.

Growth isn't always visible,
but with each challenge,
you are becoming a fuller,
truer version of yourself.

"Beyond the Seed"

For as long as she could remember, Mia had played it safe. She worked a stable job, maintained steady friendships, and rarely deviated from her routines. But deep down, she felt something missing, a quiet yearning for something more. One day, she stumbled upon a garden, where a single seedling was pushing through the soil, reaching for the sun. Mia felt drawn to its quiet strength, realizing that growth required moving beyond comfort.

Inspired, she started to make small changes. She signed up for a course in a field she'd always been curious about and took up a new hobby. Slowly but surely, Mia's life began to blossom. Each step she took taught her that growth isn't about grand transformations—it's about embracing small steps forward and finding courage in the journey. With each new experience, she uncovered layers of herself she hadn't known before, growing into the fullest version of who she was meant to be.

"Becoming"

I am not who I was,
Yet not quite who I'll be;
In the in-between, I rise,
Unfolding, steadily.

Through the cracks, I reach,
In each fall, I find grace;
For growth is a journey,
Not a single, hurried race.

Growth is not a race;
it's a journey of becoming,
one small step at a time.

"The New Beginning"

Daniel always feared change. He clung to routines and familiar paths, feeling safe within his comfort zone. But when a career shift disrupted his stable life, he felt forced to step into the unknown. With no clear direction, he found himself lost, questioning his worth and doubting his abilities.

One afternoon, while walking in a park, he noticed a small plant growing through a crack in the concrete. It had pushed through against all odds, thriving in an unlikely place. That little plant became a symbol of resilience for him—a reminder that growth often happens in unexpected ways.

With a renewed perspective, Daniel embraced the unknown. He signed up for courses, learned new skills, and gradually adapted to his new path. Over time, he realized that his struggles were helping him discover strengths he hadn't known he possessed. His journey was not without setbacks, but each challenge taught him that growth was about embracing change, no matter how daunting.

Growth is one of the most beautiful gifts you can give yourself. It's not about becoming someone else; it's about discovering more of who you truly are. Growth often happens quietly, in small, almost invisible steps. It may feel uncomfortable, and sometimes even painful, but remember that every stretch, every challenge is bringing you closer to your best self.

Allow yourself to evolve without rushing. Trust that each experience, each lesson, is shaping you into someone stronger, wiser, and more resilient. You are in the process of becoming, and every effort you make—no matter how small—is part of a beautiful transformation.

Let yourself grow at your own pace, honoring the journey without judgment. Know that this path, with all its twists and turns, is leading you exactly where you're meant to go.

Reflect on a time when you faced change or a challenge that felt uncomfortable.
What did you learn from that experience?
How did it help you grow?

_____

_____

_____

Choose one small action you can take this week that aligns with your personal growth. It could be trying a new hobby, reading a book on a subject that interests you, or even taking a different route on a walk.

Notice how this small shift feels and how it might open doors to further growth.

Growth is an ongoing journey, one that requires patience, courage, and self-compassion. Moving forward, remember that growth isn't always visible; sometimes, it happens in the quiet moments of reflection and self-discovery. Trust in your journey, allowing yourself to expand beyond the boundaries of familiarity and comfort.

As you continue on this path, know that every experience, every challenge, is a chance to become more aligned with your true self. Embrace each phase, knowing that growth is never wasted. Each step forward is a testament to your strength and commitment to yourself.

Keep reaching, keep becoming, and honor the path of growth with pride. You are not only becoming someone stronger but also embracing the fullness of who you are.

"Becoming Whole"

From seed to bloom, in quiet grace,
I find my rhythm, my own pace.
No rush to reach, no need to race,
In growth, I find my rightful place.

Each petal formed, each root I lay,
A testament to day by day.
For growth is slow, a gentle art,
Becoming whole, in mind and heart.

Growth is not about perfection,
but about finding the courage
to continue becoming.

Think about a moment in your life when you felt you were truly growing, even if it was uncomfortable.

What did this experience teach you about yourself?
How can you apply these lessons as you continue forward?

_____

_____

_____

Growth is a journey, not a destination. It's the gentle unfolding of who you are, layer by layer, experience by experience. It's okay if it feels slow, or if you sometimes wonder if you're making any progress. Growth isn't always visible; it often happens quietly, in moments of reflection, change, and discovery.

Remember, each small step you take is part of your unique path. Trust that with each experience, you're becoming more aligned with the person you're meant to be. Growth doesn't mean never making mistakes; it means learning from each one and continuing forward with courage.

Be patient with yourself, and embrace the journey as it is. You are growing every day, and with each step, you're creating a life that's true to you.

Choose one small way to step out of your comfort zone this week. It could be trying something new, taking a different perspective, or reaching out to someone you haven't connected with in a while.

Embrace this small change as a step toward growth.

Growth is a beautiful, unfolding journey that requires both patience and courage. Moving forward, remember that growth doesn't have to be quick or dramatic. It's found in the quiet moments of reflection, in each new experience, and in the willingness to try again after setbacks.

As you embrace this journey, honor the pace that feels right for you. Growth isn't about reaching an endpoint; it's about becoming more aligned with your authentic self, uncovering new strengths, and finding peace in the process. Let each step forward remind you that you are evolving, one day at a time, and that this journey is uniquely yours.

Walk forward with an open heart, knowing that each experience, each challenge, and each joy is shaping you into the person you are meant to be. Embrace growth with grace, and continue becoming, moment by moment.

Growth is not about
becoming someone else;
it's about unveiling more
of who you truly are.

"The Blooming Path"

Nina had always wanted to be a painter, but life had taken her down different paths. After years of routine, she decided to enroll in a weekend art class, not expecting much but hoping for a small change. At first, she felt awkward and hesitant, her hands unsure as they moved across the canvas. But as she kept painting, something shifted. She realized that growth wasn't about producing a masterpiece; it was about letting herself explore and try without judgment.

Each week, Nina noticed more confidence and freedom in her strokes. Her growth wasn't just in her skills but in her ability to see herself differently, to trust her own journey. She learned that growth is like a flower blooming—not rushed or forced, but nurtured with patience and care. Nina understood that each step was a brushstroke in the bigger picture of her life, adding depth and color to who she was becoming.

"Unfolding"

In time's embrace, I find my way,
Unfolding gently, day by day.
With roots that reach, with branches wide,
I grow with strength and peace inside.

No need to rush, no race to win,
I bloom with patience deep within.
For growth is slow, a quiet art,
A gentle journey of the heart.

Allow yourself to grow
at your own pace.
There's no rush;
trust that every step
is part of your journey.

Reflect on a recent challenge that made you feel stretched or uncertain.

What did this experience teach you about yourself? How has it contributed to your growth?

_____

_____

_____

friend,

Growth is a beautiful, ongoing journey. It doesn't happen in leaps or bounds; it's found in small, steady steps, in the moments of courage when you allow yourself to try something new. Remember, growth isn't about perfection; it's about exploring, learning, and letting yourself evolve without judgment.

Honor where you are in your journey, knowing that every experience adds depth to your story. Embrace each lesson, each challenge, as a stepping stone to a more authentic you. Growth doesn't require you to have all the answers; it only asks for your openness, your willingness to see what you're capable of.

Take pride in your growth, however it appears. You are blossoming in your own time, beautifully and uniquely.

With encouragement,

bestie

Take a small step toward something you've always wanted to try but haven't yet explored. It could be a hobby, a class, or a new experience.

What will it be?

_____

_____

_____

Now notice how it feels to embrace growth with curiosity rather than pressure.

Growth is a journey of gentle discovery, a path that unfolds with patience, curiosity, and courage. Moving forward, remember that growth isn't a race; it's a personal journey that honors your pace and uniqueness. Trust in the process, knowing that each step, however small, is a part of becoming who you're meant to be.

As you continue, let growth be your guide, helping you explore new perspectives, uncover hidden strengths, and embrace change. Allow each experience to add depth to your journey, knowing that growth is not about who you were or who you'll be but about the beauty of becoming.

Step forward with a heart open to growth, and trust in the power of each moment to shape your life. Embrace this journey, and know that you are blossoming in exactly the right time.

# FORGIVNESS

*HEALING (of) HEARTS*

Forgiveness is a gift of freedom—an invitation to release the weight of resentment and hurt. This chapter explores the journey of forgiving yourself and others, showing how letting go can bring clarity, healing, and a sense of peace. Through reflective prompts and letters, you'll be guided to examine old wounds and gently release them. The goal of this chapter is to help you move forward with a heart that is lighter, understanding that forgiveness is not for others, but a path to your own inner peace.

"Letting Go"

I release the chains, I shed the weight,
No longer bound by hurt or hate.
I choose to heal, to walk anew,
With open heart and skies of blue.
Forgiveness is the key I hold,
To free myself, to be whole.
Not for them, but for my peace,
I let it go, I find release.

Forgiveness can feel like one of the hardest choices to make, especially when pain and betrayal run deep. But forgiveness is a gift you give to yourself—it's a decision to no longer be held captive by the past. It's not about forgetting or excusing what happened; it's about reclaiming your energy and peace.

As you consider forgiveness, remember that it doesn't have to happen all at once. It's okay if it takes time and effort. Be gentle with yourself, allowing healing to unfold naturally. Each small step you take toward forgiveness is a step toward freedom, a chance to open your heart to peace.

Know that you deserve to live fully and joyfully, free from the burdens of resentment. Choose forgiveness for yourself, and watch how it transforms your world.

"A Step Toward Freedom"

Jenna had carried resentment for years. An old friend had betrayed her trust, and although the friendship had ended, the hurt lingered. Every time Jenna thought of her friend, a wave of anger and sadness washed over her. She realized this bitterness was keeping her trapped in the past, unable to move forward.

One day, Jenna decided to write a letter to her friend—not to send, but simply to release her feelings. She poured her heart out, expressing her pain and her wish to let go. By the end, she felt lighter, as if a weight had been lifted. Jenna realized that forgiveness wasn't about condoning what had happened; it was about freeing herself from the grip of the past.

Over time, as she revisited that choice, she noticed how much more peace she had within herself. Her act of forgiveness became a step toward freedom, allowing her to reclaim her energy and focus on her own happiness.

Forgiveness is not about forgetting;
it's about freeing yourself
to live fully once again.

Think about someone you may need to forgive, whether it's yourself or someone else. Reflect on how holding onto this hurt affects you. How might letting go create more peace in your life?

_____

_____

_____

Write a letter expressing your feelings of hurt, betrayal, or anger toward someone you need to forgive (even if it's yourself).
You don't need to send it; just use this letter as a way to release the emotions you've been holding onto.

The Freedom of Forgiveness

Forgiveness is a journey of courage and self-compassion. Moving forward, remember that forgiving is not about denying your feelings or ignoring your pain. It's about acknowledging what happened and choosing to release its hold on you. As you walk this path, know that forgiveness is a powerful way to honor yourself and reclaim your peace.

Letting go is not a sign of weakness; it's a declaration of strength. It's a way of saying that you deserve to live free, unburdened by resentment. Embrace this freedom, knowing that each act of forgiveness makes room for new experiences, new joys, and deeper peace within yourself.

Continue forward with grace, knowing that forgiveness allows you to live fully and freely. Embrace this journey of letting go, and welcome the abundance of love, joy, and healing that awaits you.

Forgiveness isn't
letting go of the past

it's freeing yourself to
fully live in the present.

"The Bridge to Peace"

After years of silence, Laura received a message from an old friend who had hurt her deeply. The message brought back a flood of memories—both the joy they'd shared and the pain that had ended their friendship. Although she had moved on, she realized she was still carrying the weight of unresolved resentment.

Laura took a walk by a river near her home, and as she crossed a small bridge, she felt something shift within her. She imagined leaving her anger behind on one side of the bridge, choosing peace as she crossed to the other. Laura understood that forgiveness was not about forgetting or reconciling; it was about releasing herself from the grip of the past. She felt a weight lift, as if she'd created space within herself to breathe freely again.

With each step forward, Laura embraced the freedom that came from forgiveness. She learned that forgiveness is a bridge to peace, allowing her to carry only what served her in the present.

Consider a situation or person you still feel resentment toward. How has holding onto this feeling affected your life?
Imagine what it would feel like to release this burden.
What might you gain by forgiving?

_____

_____

_____

"A Release"

I free the chains that bound my heart,
And let the pain and hurt depart.
Forgiveness flows, a gentle breeze,
In letting go, I find my peace.

No longer tied to past regret,
I choose to heal, to not forget.
For I am free, unburdened, whole,
Forgiveness soothes my weary soul.

Forgiveness is the gift of
peace you give to yourself.
Let go, not for them,
but to set yourself free.

dear reader,

forgiveness is a gift you give yourself, a path to peace and freedom. It's natural to feel resistance toward forgiving, especially when the hurt runs deep. But forgiveness is not about erasing the past or denying your pain. It's about releasing the hold that anger and resentment have over your heart.

imagine the weight lifting as you let go, as you choose to set yourself free. Forgiveness doesn't mean you have to forget, reconcile, or excuse anyone's actions. It simply allows you to reclaim your energy and create space for healing.

take each step at your own pace. Remember, you deserve peace. Forgiveness is a powerful way to honor yourself, to move forward with an open heart, and to let go of what no longer serves you.

with compassion,

he whom also walks this journey

Write a letter to yourself or to someone who hurt you, expressing everything you've held onto. You don't need to send it; this is for your own healing. Let it be a release, a way to free yourself from the weight of the past.

_____

_____

_____

_____

_____

_____

_____

_____

_____

_____

_____

Forgiveness is the gentle act of
releasing the weight that holds
you back from peace.

The Freedom in Forgiveness

Forgiveness is a gentle path that leads to freedom, a reminder that you hold the power to heal and release what no longer serves you. Moving forward, remember that forgiveness is a choice made for yourself. It is an act of courage that allows you to move forward without the weight of the past.

As you walk this journey, trust in your strength to let go and find peace. Embrace forgiveness as a bridge to healing, a way to reclaim your energy and live fully in the present. You deserve a life unburdened by resentment, a heart that is open and free.

Continue forward with grace, knowing that forgiveness is a path to peace, a way to honor your own journey. Let each step remind you of the beauty and freedom in choosing to forgive.

"The Gift of Letting Go"

After a long friendship had ended in betrayal, Keira found herself holding onto resentment. The anger she felt was like a constant companion, reminding her of the pain she'd endured. She convinced herself that holding onto this feeling would somehow protect her from being hurt again.

One day, while visiting a nearby lake, she noticed how rocks skipped across the water, leaving ripples before they sank. She picked up a small stone, imagining it was the weight of her resentment. As she threw it into the lake, she felt a surprising sense of release. Keira realized that forgiveness wasn't for her former friend; it was a gift she could give herself. By letting go, she freed herself from carrying the weight of the past.

From that day forward, whenever she felt the anger resurface, she'd remember the feeling of that stone leaving her hand, the ripples in the water, and the sense of peace she'd found in choosing to release what no longer served her.

You don't have to forget to forgive.
Release the weight and allow
yourself to move forward.

"Unburdened"

With open hands, I let it fall,
The weight that held me tight and small.
In gentle grace, I choose release,
In letting go, I find my peace.

No chains to bind, no grudge to bear,
Forgiveness flows like open air.
For I am free, my spirit light,
Unburdened now, in morning's light.

Consider someone or something you feel ready to forgive, even if it's yourself. How might releasing this resentment bring you more peace? What would you gain by choosing to let go?

_____

_____

_____

to the part of me that is finally ready to forgive,

forgiveness is a quiet, yet profound act of self-compassion. It's not about condoning what happened or erasing the past; it's about freeing yourself from the hold that resentment has over your heart. Forgiveness is a way to let go of what no longer serves you, creating space for peace and healing.

remember, forgiveness is a journey, one that takes time and patience. Be gentle with yourself as you walk this path. Each step you take toward forgiveness is a step toward reclaiming your joy and lightness. It's a choice to live fully, to unburden yourself from the past, and to embrace the freedom that lies ahead.

trust in your capacity to forgive, and know that it will lead you to a place of peace and clarity.

with compassion,

the part of you thats finally moved on

Find a small object, like a pebble or a leaf, to represent the weight of your resentment. Hold it in your hand and reflect on the hurt it represents, then release it in a place that brings you peace—a river, a lake, or even a garden. Let this act symbolize your choice to let go.

The Freedom in Forgiveness

Forgiveness is a journey of release, a decision to set yourself free from the weight of the past. Moving forward, let forgiveness be your path to peace, a gentle reminder that you are worthy of living unburdened by resentment. Trust that by letting go, you make space for healing, growth, and joy.

As you continue on this journey, remember that forgiveness is a gift you give to yourself, an act of courage that opens the door to new beginnings. Embrace this freedom, allowing it to fill you with lightness and hope. Walk forward with a heart unburdened, and let forgiveness lead you to a place of lasting peace.

# HOPE

*HEALING (of) HEARTS*

Hope is Finding Light in Moments of Darkness.

Hope is the quiet strength that sustains us, even when life feels uncertain. In this chapter, you'll find reminders of the small but powerful ways hope can be a lifeline in difficult times. Through stories of transformation and moments of faith, you'll be encouraged to look for light, even in the darkest of places. By the end of this chapter, you'll come to understand that hope isn't about dismissing hardship but about trusting that better days lie ahead and that you have the courage to reach them.

Hope is the light that guides
us through the darkest nights,
a reminder that dawn always follows.

Think about a difficult time when you felt hopeless but eventually saw a change for the better. What helped you through that time? How can you hold onto hope in your current circumstances?

_____

_____

_____

"The Candle in the Dark"

Marcus had faced one struggle after another. He lost his job, his relationship ended, and his family was far away. There were nights he felt swallowed by despair, wondering if things would ever change. One particularly hard night, he found himself wandering into a small, quiet church, where a single candle flickered in the corner.

As he stared at the flame, a strange comfort washed over him. That small light, though fragile, was steady, unwavering against the darkness. Marcus realized that hope was like that candle—small, perhaps, but powerful enough to illuminate even the darkest room.

From that night on, whenever he felt overwhelmed, he'd close his eyes and imagine that candle, burning brightly. In time, things began to shift. Small opportunities appeared, people came into his life to lend support, and he found himself growing stronger, day by day. The candle remained his symbol of hope, a quiet reminder that even in his darkest moments, there was always a glimmer of light.

"Dawn"

In the silence of the night, I wait,
For whispers of a kinder fate.
Though darkness cloaks the weary sky,
I hold to hope; dawn is nigh.

For every shadow hides a spark,
A light that glows against the dark.
In patient faith, I lift my gaze,
And greet the sun's returning rays.

to the beautiful soul that is you,

hope is often the quiet strength that carries us through. It doesn't shout or demand attention; it's the gentle reminder that better days are coming. When life feels overwhelming, it can be hard to hold onto hope, but even the smallest glimmer can guide us forward.

no matter what you're facing, know that hope can be found in the simplest things—a kind word, a small victory, or a beautiful sunrise. Let these moments remind you that life is constantly moving, constantly changing. Your hardships will pass, and new doors will open.

hold onto hope, even if it's only a tiny flicker. Trust that each step forward brings you closer to the light. You are resilient, and your story is still unfolding.

- an admirer

Hope is a small but steady
light in the darkness.
Even a flicker can guide you forward.

Each evening for the next week, write down one small thing that brings you hope—a goal, a dream, a kind interaction, or a comforting thought. Let these daily reminders become your "candle," guiding you through any darkness you may face.

Day 1: _____

Day 2: _____

Day 3: _____

Day 4: _____

Day 5: _____

Day 6: _____

Day 7: _____

Guided by Hope

Hope is a steady, gentle presence in our lives, a quiet reminder that change is always possible. Moving forward, remember that hope doesn't need to be grand or bold. It can be as small as a whisper, a flicker of light, enough to guide you through the moments when life feels uncertain.

As you continue on your journey, allow hope to be your anchor, your guiding light. Trust that even in the midst of challenges, brighter days are ahead. Embrace hope as a companion that walks beside you, a reminder that life is filled with possibilities waiting to be discovered.

Keep your eyes on the light, however small it may seem, and let hope be the foundation upon which you build your dreams. Move forward with courage, and let your heart be filled with the promise of new beginnings.

"The Small Light"

Aiden had been through a difficult year. A series of setbacks had left him feeling lost, uncertain, and drained of optimism. One night, while walking in his neighborhood, he noticed a small candle flickering in a neighbor's window. Drawn to its warm glow, Aiden stopped to take in the peaceful light, realizing how something so small could pierce the darkness.

Inspired, he began lighting a candle every evening, letting it represent the hope he wanted to cultivate within himself. Over time, Aiden found comfort in this simple ritual. The candle reminded him that hope doesn't need to be grand or overpowering; it only needs to be present, steady enough to guide him through each day.

In time, Aiden's outlook began to shift. Small opportunities appeared, and he began to reconnect with the strength he thought he had lost. The candlelight became his quiet symbol of resilience, reminding him that hope could illuminate his path, no matter how dark it seemed.

"A Spark"

In shadows deep, I find my way,
A spark of hope to light the gray.
With gentle glow, it warms my heart,
A promise that's both fierce and smart.

Though winds may howl and storms may rise,
This quiet hope, it never dies.
For in its glow, I see the dawn,
And find the strength to carry on.

hope is often a quiet, gentle force, one that may seem small but holds incredible power. When life feels uncertain or challenging, hope becomes the light that helps you see beyond the darkness. It doesn't have to be loud or grand; sometimes, a single spark is enough to guide you forward.

remember, hope is within you, ready to shine whenever you need it. Look for it in the small moments—the kindness of a friend, the beauty of a sunset, or the quiet moments of peace. These are reminders that life is full of possibilities, even in the hardest times.

hold onto hope with both hands, knowing that each step you take, no matter how small, is a step toward brighter days. Let hope be the light that guides you, a steady flame reminding you of your strength.

from,

me

Think of a time when you felt hopeless but later experienced a positive change. What helped you hold onto hope during that period? How can you use this memory to inspire hope in your current life?

_____

_____

_____

Hope is a quiet light,
steady and true,
guiding us forward,
even when the path is unclear.

Embracing Hope as a Guide

Hope is the quiet, unwavering light that can lead you through any challenge. Moving forward, let hope be the gentle guide that reminds you of your resilience and strength. Hope doesn't erase difficulties but offers a path through them, a promise that there's light on the other side.

As you continue this journey, embrace hope as a companion, a reminder that change is always possible. Allow it to be the steady flame that brightens your path, helping you move forward with courage and faith.

Hold onto hope, knowing that it has the power to transform, uplift, and renew. Each day is a new beginning, filled with possibilities waiting to unfold. Embrace each step with hope as your guide, trusting in the beauty of all that lies ahead.

For the next week, start each morning by writing down one thing you're hopeful for, no matter how big or small. Let these hopes remind you of the possibilities that each day brings.

Day 1: _____

Day 2: _____

Day 3: _____

Day 4: _____

Day 5: _____

Day 6: _____

Day 7: _____

Hope is the belief
that there is light,
even if we can't yet see it.

"The Candle's Glow"

When Emma lost her job, she felt as though her whole world had collapsed. Each day felt heavy, and she struggled to see a way forward. One evening, as she was tidying her apartment, she found an old candle tucked away in a drawer. Without much thought, she lit it, watching the small flame flicker gently in the dim room.

As she stared at the flame, something within her softened. She realized that, even in the darkest moments, a small light could change everything. Emma decided to let the candle become her symbol of hope—a reminder that, no matter how bleak things seemed, there was always the potential for new beginnings. She lit the candle each evening, finding solace in its glow and renewing her belief that change was on the horizon.

In time, Emma's circumstances improved, but she never forgot the power of that tiny flame. The candle had shown her that hope wasn't about certainty but about the quiet trust that light would return, one way or another.

"Flicker of Light"

A spark, a flame, a glow so small,
Yet in the dark, it guides us all.
In quiet warmth, it shines anew,
A gentle promise, pure and true.

Though shadows fall and nights are long,
Hope is the whisper, soft yet strong.
A flicker bright, in endless night,
A steady hand, a source of light.

to my curly hair'd sis,

hope is often a soft, quiet presence, a gentle reminder that no matter what, there's always the potential for light. Life may bring unexpected storms, times when the way forward feels uncertain, but hope is the anchor that holds you steady, the promise that this moment, too, will pass.

when things feel heavy, look for small sources of light—comforting words, acts of kindness, or even a simple moment of peace. These small glimmers are reminders that hope lives within you, ready to guide you through each challenge.

allow yourself to hold onto hope, even when it feels faint. Trust that brighter days lie ahead and that you have the courage to walk toward them.

with warmth and faith,

 - your curly haired brother

Reflect on a time when you found hope in an unexpected place. What did this moment teach you about your ability to keep moving forward? How can you hold onto this memory in difficult times?

_____

_____

_____

Walking in Hope's Light

Hope is the quiet flame that keeps you moving forward, a gentle assurance that, no matter how dark the night, morning will come. Moving forward, let hope be your guide, a reminder that you can face any challenge with the belief that light is waiting on the other side.

As you walk this journey, know that hope will be with you, steady and unwavering. Trust in its power to lift you, to give you courage, and to carry you through any storm. Embrace hope as a lifelong companion, a gentle source of strength that reminds you to keep moving forward.

Step forward with a heart full of hope, knowing that brighter days are ahead. Hold onto this light, and let it guide you, one step at a time, toward all that awaits.

In the hardest moments,
hold onto hope.
It may be quiet,
but it has the power to lift
you higher than you realize.

Choose an item that represents hope to you—a candle, a stone, or a flower. Keep it somewhere visible as a reminder that, even in dark moments, hope is always within reach. Take a few minutes each day to focus on this object and let it renew your belief in brighter days.

Day 1: _____

Day 2: _____

Day 3: _____

Day 4: _____

Day 5: _____

Day 6: _____

Day 7: _____

# HEALING (of) HEARTS

# ACCEPTANCE

Acceptance is embracing the Present Moment as it is.

Acceptance is a profound step toward inner peace, allowing you to fully embrace where you are and who you are in this moment. This chapter guides you through the process of letting go of resistance and finding beauty in your present self and circumstances. Through poetry, letters, and prompts, you'll be encouraged to release the need for perfection and find grace in the journey. The end goal of this chapter is to cultivate a gentle self-acceptance, helping you approach life with ease and a sense of wholeness.

In accepting who we are
and where we stand,
we find the power
to grow beyond our limits.

"A New Perspective"

Renee had always struggled to accept her journey. She compared herself to others, feeling as if her progress was somehow "less than." Her friends seemed to have it all together—stable careers, relationships, even families—while she was still finding her way.

One day, while hiking, she reached a high point overlooking a vast landscape. For a moment, all her insecurities faded, and she simply stood in awe of the view before her. Renee realized that each tree, river, and hill had its own beauty, and none needed to be compared. She thought, "Why can't I see my journey this way?"

Over time, Renee practiced accepting herself exactly as she was, learning to view her unique path with compassion and appreciation. Her journey didn't need to look like anyone else's to be valuable. She found peace in accepting her own story and realized that true growth begins with loving where you are, no matter how far you still want to go.

"Just as I Am"

I need not change, to earn my grace,
For here I stand, in time and space.
With flaws and scars, and all I bring,
I am enough, a living thing.

Acceptance blooms, a gentle truth,
A tender gift, eternal youth.
I grow with love, in present tense,
And find my strength in acceptance.

my dear sponsee,

acceptance is one of the most beautiful and freeing gifts you can offer yourself. It doesn't mean you're giving up or settling; it means you're choosing peace with who you are and where you are right now. It's about acknowledging that every part of your journey has a purpose, even if it's not clear yet.

embrace yourself with kindness, recognizing that perfection is not the goal— progress is. Your experiences, your strengths, your challenges all make up the beautiful, unique person that you are. By accepting yourself and your path, you open the door to even greater growth and healing.

know that you are exactly where you're meant to be, and that embracing this moment can be the foundation for all the change and growth you desire.

now pick yourself up, dust yourself off and get back to work.

i stand proud of your progress and have faith in where you go next ...

- your sponsor

Think of a part of yourself or your life
that you struggle to accept.

Reflect on how accepting this aspect,
rather than resisting it, might create
more peace or ease in your life.

The Power of Acceptance

Acceptance is not an endpoint; it's a stepping stone toward true peace and growth. As you continue forward, remember that accepting yourself and your journey as it is today doesn't limit you. It empowers you. When you embrace who you are and where you stand, you release the pressure to "become" and allow yourself to simply "be."

Moving forward, let acceptance be a reminder that life is not a race or a competition but a personal journey. Each moment of acceptance builds a stronger foundation, helping you to grow, heal, and become the fullest version of yourself. Embrace acceptance as an invitation to find peace and joy in the present, and let it lead you to a future filled with grace.

Step forward with love, knowing that you are already enough, just as you are.

Acceptance is not giving up;
it's making peace with what is.
Embrace the present and find
your balance.

Each day for the next week, write down one thing you appreciate about yourself or your journey. It can be something simple, like resilience, creativity, or kindness.

Let this practice help you cultivate acceptance and gratitude for who you are today.

Day 1: _____

Day 2: _____

Day 3: _____

Day 4: _____

Day 5: _____

Day 6: _____

Day 7: _____

In accepting what is,

we find the strength to grow,
the peace to heal
and the courage to move forward.

"The Gift of the Present"

For years, Carla struggled with wishing her life were different. She was constantly comparing herself to others, imagining how much happier she'd be if only her circumstances would change. One day, her grandmother, who had lived a life full of joy despite her challenges, shared a bit of wisdom: "Sometimes the secret to happiness is simply accepting where you are."

Carla decided to try. She began to focus on the present moment, choosing to embrace her reality rather than resist it. She practiced gratitude for the small things and discovered beauty in her everyday life. Over time, her restlessness faded, replaced by a newfound peace. Carla realized that acceptance wasn't about settling; it was about finding harmony with her path, allowing her to grow with grace and courage.

"In This Moment"

I release the need to change my pace,
I find my peace in this time and place.
With open heart and mind at ease,
I let my worries gently cease.

For in this moment, I am whole,
Acceptance frees my restless soul.
No need to fix, no need to flee,
For I am enough, and I am free.

Acceptance is a gentle act of love, a way to honor yourself and your journey. It's not about giving up or resigning to your circumstances; it's about embracing where you are and finding peace within it. Acceptance is the bridge between who you are and who you are becoming.

Life may not always look the way we imagine, but that doesn't mean it lacks beauty or purpose. By choosing acceptance, you allow yourself to experience each moment fully, without the need for constant change or control. Acceptance is a gift you give yourself, one that brings calm, clarity, and strength.

Take a deep breath, let go of expectations, and remember that you are exactly where you are meant to be. Trust in this moment, knowing that acceptance opens the door to growth and peace.

The present moment holds beauty,
even if it's not perfect.
Accept where you are as a stepping
stone to where you're going.

Consider a part of your life or a trait in yourself that you've struggled to accept. What would it feel like to embrace this fully, without judgment? How might this shift bring more peace?

_____

_____

_____

Finding Freedom in Acceptance

Acceptance is a journey that leads to peace, allowing you to embrace yourself and your life as they are. Moving forward, let acceptance remind you that you don't need to change or control everything to find fulfillment. Instead, you can find harmony by trusting that every step, every moment, is shaping you.

As you continue on this path, allow acceptance to bring you closer to your true self. Embrace each experience, each feeling, without judgment or resistance. This is where freedom lives—within the peace of accepting what is.

Walk forward with grace, knowing that acceptance will guide you with patience and compassion. Let it open doors to growth, healing, and an inner harmony that empowers you to live fully and beautifully.

Acceptance is the peaceful
acknowledgment of what is,
allowing us to find ease
within the moment.

Each evening, with kindness, take a few minutes to write down something from your day that you can accept just as it is.

Let this practice help you find peace and appreciation in the present moment.

Day 1: _____

Day 2: _____

Day 3: _____

Day 4: _____

Day 5: _____

Day 6: _____

Day 7: _____

"Embracing the Present"

Jackson had always been someone who planned every detail of his life. But after a series of unexpected changes—a breakup, a job shift, and moving to a new city —he felt as though his plans had crumbled. He kept wishing things were different, wanting his life to look like he'd imagined.

One evening, while out for a walk, he came across a small garden filled with wildflowers, each growing at its own angle, bending and twisting toward the light. Jackson realized these flowers weren't perfect or planted in neat rows, yet each one added beauty in its own way. In that moment, he understood that acceptance was about embracing things as they were, not as he wished them to be.

Jackson began practicing acceptance, letting go of his need to control every detail and allowing himself to find peace with the present. Over time, he learned that acceptance wasn't about settling but about finding beauty and purpose in each moment, exactly as it was.

"Flowing with Grace"

I let go of the need to mold,
To change, to fix, to grasp, to hold.
In gentle peace, I find my place,
Embracing life, flowing with grace.

No struggle here, no war to win,
Acceptance blooms in soft within.
For in this calm, I come to see,
Life's beauty flows through being free.

to me -

acceptance is a gift you give to yourself—a way of finding peace within, even if life doesn't look exactly as you imagined. It's about embracing each moment without judgment, allowing yourself to let go of the need for perfection and control.

remember, acceptance doesn't mean you have to settle or stop striving for change. It simply means honoring the present, finding grace in what is, and releasing the struggle against what cannot be changed. With acceptance, you create space for growth, for peace, and for greater understanding.

allow yourself to rest in the knowledge that everything is unfolding as it's meant to, and trust that you are exactly where you need to be.

- from me

Consider an area of your life where you often feel resistance. How would it feel to approach this part of your life with acceptance instead? What might shift if you allow yourself to let go of control?

_____

_____

_____

Practice mindful acceptance by choosing one part of your day to fully embrace just as it is. Whether it's your morning routine, a conversation, or a quiet moment, allow yourself to experience it without judgment or a need for change.

Notice how this brings a sense of peace.

The Peace of Acceptance

Acceptance is a gentle, powerful way of embracing life as it is, creating space for both peace and growth. Moving forward, let acceptance be your grounding force, guiding you to find calm in each moment. Trust that, by accepting what is, you allow life to unfold naturally and beautifully.

As you continue on this journey, remember that acceptance isn't about giving up; it's about finding harmony within the present and letting go of the need for constant control. This peaceful surrender opens the door to true joy and freedom.

Walk forward with a heart full of acceptance, and let it guide you with grace and compassion. Embrace life's moments as they come, and know that in acceptance lies the strength to live fully and beautifully.

>>>

*HEALING (of) HEARTS*

# COMPASSION

Compassion is the warmth and understanding we bring to ourselves and others in moments of difficulty. This chapter invites you to cultivate a compassionate heart, teaching you to approach yourself and those around you with kindness, patience, and empathy. Through stories, poems, letters, and reflective prompts, you'll be guided to embrace compassion as a powerful tool for healing, connection, and resilience. The goal of this chapter is to help you foster a deep sense of empathy and understanding, creating a life grounded in kindness, both inwardly and outwardly.

Compassion is the quiet strength
that invites understanding,
acceptance, and love into
every moment."

"The Heart's Embrace"

Sophia had always been hard on herself, especially when things didn't go as planned. After an exhausting week at work, she came home feeling defeated and frustrated with herself for not meeting every goal. As she was walking her dog that evening, she saw a young child trip and fall, and instinctively, she felt a surge of kindness. She offered a smile and encouraging words, helping the child up.

In that moment, Sophia realized that she rarely extended the same kindness toward herself. She understood that compassion wasn't just something to offer others; it was something she could give to herself as well. From that day on, she practiced talking to herself like a friend, with gentleness and understanding. Sophia discovered that compassion brought peace to her inner world, allowing her to approach life's challenges with greater resilience.

For the whole day, practice self-compassion by speaking kindly to yourself. Whenever you notice self-criticism, replace it with an encouraging phrase or a gentle reminder that you are doing your best.

List a few of the phrases below. Reflect on your growth throughout the day.

_____

_____

_____

_____

_____

_____

Practice this exercise as often as needed.

Compassion begins within.
Treat yourself with the
understanding and kindness
you so readily give others.

"A Gentle Hand"

With gentle heart, I meet my soul,
With kindness deep, I am made whole.
No harsh demand, no voice of blame,
In love, I call myself by name.

For in this peace, I find my way,
Through darkened night and brightened day.
Compassion flows, a healing balm,
A gift of grace, a gentle calm.

Compassion is the quiet gift of love, a way of holding yourself and others in kindness, even when things feel difficult. It means seeing yourself not with criticism but with understanding, offering yourself the same patience you would give a friend.

When life feels overwhelming, compassion can be the gentlest balm, a reminder that you don't need to be perfect to be worthy of love. Approach yourself with kindness, offering words of encouragement rather than judgment. And let this compassion flow outward, allowing it to connect you more deeply with others.

Compassion invites healing, forgiveness, and peace. By embracing it, you give yourself permission to be human, to grow, and to feel supported every step of the way.

Reflect on a recent moment when you were critical of yourself. How might compassion have changed the way you felt in that moment? How can you practice speaking to yourself with more kindness?

_____

_____

_____

Living with Compassion

Compassion is the heart's way of inviting peace, healing, and understanding into every moment. Moving forward, let compassion be your guiding light, a reminder that kindness is a powerful force—one that heals both yourself and those around you.

As you continue this journey, allow compassion to be the voice within that soothes, encourages, and forgives. Let it be the bridge between resilience and acceptance, self-love and hope. Embrace compassion as a way of honoring yourself and others, knowing that this kindness will always light the way forward.

Walk with a heart full of compassion, allowing it to shape your journey with grace, strength, and love.

Compassion is the
kindness that softens
our edges, making space
for healing and connection.

"A New Understanding"

Carlos had always been quick to judge himself, particularly when he made mistakes. He'd replay situations over and over, critiquing every word, every action. One day, he found himself at a community event, watching as a volunteer patiently helped an elderly woman who'd spilled her coffee. Instead of frustration, the volunteer offered her a smile and a few kind words.

Carlos realized that he rarely offered himself the same patience and understanding he saw in that simple moment. Inspired, he decided to practice self-compassion, reminding himself that everyone makes mistakes and that kindness could transform his perspective. Over time, Carlos found that approaching himself with understanding brought a sense of peace and resilience he hadn't known before.

"Kind Words"

With kind words soft, I meet my heart,
A gentleness, a brand new start.
No need to strive, no need to prove,
In love, I find my place, my groove.

For in compassion's gentle light,
I ease my load, I find what's right.
A friend to self, a soothing balm,
Compassion's touch, a steady calm.

my heart -

you thought me that compassion is the gift of understanding, a way to meet ourselves and others with an open heart. You've thought me that it's easy to be critical, especially when things go wrong, but true strength lies in approaching those moments with kindness.

you've taught me that when I take a moment to treat myself how I would treat you, life becomes easier. You've taught me that even our tough times become learning moments - challenges become opportunities for growth. Your compassion has helped me embrace this journey without harsh judgment while inviting healing and peace into my life.

you remind me everyday that I am are worthy of kindness—especially my own.

with all my heart

- your husband

Reflect on a recent situation where you felt judgmental toward yourself or others. How might compassion have changed this experience? What would it look like to approach similar situations with empathy?

_____

_____

_____

Each morning of this week, this week, write yourself an encouraging note. Write this note out and post on your mirror, refrigerator, desk - anywhere you are certain to see it. Each morning, practice a few minutes of gentle breathing as you read this note allowing the words to sink in softly, gently and resonating with love.

Let this ritual remind you of the compassion you deserve.

What does each note say?

Day 1:_____

Day 2:_____

Day 3:_____

Day 4:_____

Day 5:_____

Day 6:_____

Day 7:_____

Compassion as a Path to Peace

Compassion is a way of bringing peace into each moment, a practice of extending kindness to yourself and others. Moving forward, let compassion guide your journey, reminding you that it's okay to make mistakes, to feel, and to grow. Compassion is not just an action but a way of being—a path to understanding and connecting deeply with the world around you.

As you continue on this path, embrace compassion as a source of strength and resilience. Allow it to create a space for healing, for forgiveness, and for growth. Walk forward with a compassionate heart, knowing that each act of kindness brings more peace to your life and to the lives of others.

Compassion is the
warmth of the heart
that brings comfort
and light to the
darkest of days.

"Extending the Light"

Maya had always been the caretaker for her friends and family, always ready to offer a helping hand and a listening ear. But when it came to herself, she was quick to ignore her own needs, convinced that asking for help was a sign of weakness. One day, after a particularly rough week, her best friend noticed Maya's exhaustion and reminded her, "It's okay to be kind to yourself, too."

That simple reminder changed everything. Maya started taking small steps to care for herself, realizing that compassion wasn't something to reserve only for others. She learned that by extending the light of compassion inward, she could approach life with a fuller heart, ready to support herself just as she did everyone else.

Compassion is the warmth we can extend to ourselves, especially in moments of struggle. It's easy to reserve kindness for others, but true compassion includes caring for yourself with the same gentle understanding.

When life feels difficult, remind yourself that you deserve love, too. Compassion allows you to be human, to grow, and to learn without the burden of perfection. Let it be a source of strength and a reminder that you are worthy of kindness and care.

Allow compassion to be a steady light in your life, illuminating a path forward that feels both peaceful and empowering.

"Softly Held"

In gentle arms, I hold my soul,
A tender care, a heart made whole.
No rush to fix, no need to mend,
In compassion's grace, I am my friend.

I meet myself with warmth and light,
In darkest days, I find what's right.
Compassion's glow, a steady flame,
With love I call myself by name.

When you meet yourself
with compassion, you create a safe
space for healing, growth, and peace.

Think of a time when you were quick to help someone in need. What would it look like to offer that same kindness and support to yourself? How might this shift the way you view self-compassion?

_____

_____

_____

Create a small compassion jar. Each time you do something kind for yourself—whether it's resting, speaking kindly to yourself, or listening to your needs—add a small note to the jar.

At the end of a week, reflect on all the ways you practiced compassion toward yourself.

Carrying Compassion's Light

Compassion is a quiet yet powerful strength, a light that brightens the path forward. Moving ahead, let compassion be a way of life, a gentle reminder that kindness can heal and uplift. By extending compassion to yourself and others, you create a life filled with understanding, patience, and peace.

As you continue, allow compassion to be your guide through both the joyful and difficult moments. Let it be the steady warmth that keeps you grounded, reminding you that each step forward is a chance to offer love—to yourself and to the world around you. Walk forward with a compassionate heart, knowing that kindness has the power to transform everything it touches.

# EPILOGUE

As you reach the final pages of HEALING (of) HEARTS, take a moment to breathe and honor the journey you've traveled. This book was created as a gentle companion—a place of comfort, hope, and reflection for the moments when life feels challenging, and for the quiet times when you seek solace within yourself.

Each story, poem, reflection, and letter was crafted with the intention of offering you a safe space to feel, to heal, and to rediscover the beauty of your own heart. Healing is not a single destination but a continuous journey, an ever-unfolding path that invites you to embrace both the light and shadow within.

As you step forward, carry with you the wisdom, strength, and compassion you've nurtured here. Let these words remind you that you are whole, even in moments of brokenness, and that within you lies a resilient spirit capable of growth, peace, and love. Remember that every small step you take toward healing adds to the beauty of your story, a story uniquely yours.

Thank you for allowing HEALING (of) HEARTS to be a part of your journey. May you continue to find comfort in these pages whenever you need a reminder of your own strength, and may your heart always find its way toward hope and light.

With incredibly love, great appreciation and sincere gratitude,

Axel Jordan

thank you
&
happy healing
— axel

coming soon

HEALING (of) HEARTS
volumes
2 & 3

Other works by Axel Jordan

SON'S & SHADOWS
LOVE NOTES
365 Days Of Affirmations

coming soon,

The Journey Back
Beyond Lust

## ABOUT THE AUTHOR

Axel Jordan is a visionary musician, master certified sound healer, and certified CBT & REBT coach practitioner with a passion for helping others discover their inner strength and embrace healing. Drawing from his own transformative journey, Axel weaves together sound therapy, emotional reflection, and holistic practices to guide individuals through life's challenges with compassion and grace.

Born and raised in Brooklyn, NYC, Axel's diverse cultural and musical background shapes his deeply personal approach to well-being. In HEALING (of) HEARTS: Stories, Poems, Reflections, and Letters of Hope, Axel shares a heartfelt collection inspired by the human experience—its challenges, beauty, and capacity for resilience. Through this book, he offers readers a safe space to reflect, heal, and reconnect with the hope that lies within.

Known for his celestial alchemy sound healing and his ability to create deeply transformative experiences, Axel blends his expertise as a sound healer with his background as a coach to inspire growth and emotional connection. His work has touched the lives of countless individuals, encouraging them to approach life with kindness, self-love, and renewed purpose.

When not writing or leading sound bath healing sessions, Axel enjoys quiet moments with his partner and the animals they foster, embodying the values of love and compassion that resonate in his work. HEALING (of) HEARTS is an extension of his life's mission: to help others find peace, strength, and light, no matter where they are on their journey.

www.AxelJordanBooks.com

**Cover Design:** Axel Jordan

ISBN: 979-8-89686-146-1

Library of Congress Control Number: 2024924252

ATTENTION: SCHOOL AND BUSINESSES

Any published works of Axel Jordan are available at quantity discounts with bulk purchase for educational, business, or sales promotional use.

For information, please contact:

www.AxelJordanBooks.com